North Shore NUGGETS

Stories of Life, Love, and the Law on Lake Superior

James H. Manahan

NORTH SHORE NUGGETS
STORIES OF LIFE, LOVE, AND THE LAW ON LAKE SUPERIOR

iUniverse books may be ordered through booksellers or by contacting:

iUniverse
1663 Liberty Drive
Bloomington, IN 47403
www.iuniverse.com
1-800-Authors (1-800-288-4677)

ISBN: 978-1-4917-5477-1 (sc)
ISBN: 978-1-4917-5476-4 (e)

Library of Congress Control Number: 2014921636

Printed in the United States of America.

iUniverse rev. date: 12/05/2014

I dedicate this book to my wife Cristina,
who brought me to the North Shore

James H. Manahan on the steps of the Lake County
Courthouse, Two Harbors, Minnesota

ABOUT THE AUTHOR

After graduating from Harvard College and Harvard Law School,
James H. Manahan spent 50 years practicing law (Mankato, MN)
and teaching law. He received four Fulbright grants to teach trial skills
in South America, training students, lawyers and judges in Chile,
Argentina, Ecuador, and Costa Rica. He was named one of the "Top
10 Minnesota Attorneys of 2001" by Minnesota Lawyer newspaper.
He was President of Common Cause in Minnesota and the ACLU
of Minnesota. Now he serves as the Victim Witness Coordinator in
the Lake County Attorney's office and writes a column called Legal
Learning for Lake County. He and his wife Cristina Manahan live in
Silver Bay, Minnesota.

The articles gathered here have all been published in the Lake County
News Chronicle of Two Harbors, Minnesota. The opinions expressed
in this book are those of its author and are not to be attributed to his
employer.

CONTENTS

About the Author vii

Fascinating North Shore Cases
1   The Man Who Walks With Bears 3
2   The Case against County Attorney Tim Scannell....................6
3   Death and a Black Box on the Gunflint Trail 10
4   The Silver Bay Spur Station Condemnation Case 14
5   The Last Place on Earth is Closed 17
6   The Saga of Baby Veronica, Native American Child.............20
7   Did Lou's Fish House break the law? 23
8   Sexual Harassment in North Country Mines 26

Local Legal Legends
9   Flying Tiger Whitey: Longest Serving City Attorney
    in US History..31
10 Duluth Super-Lawyer Judge..34
11 Like Father, Like Son on the North Shore 37

Big Legal Changes Affecting the North Shore
12 PolyMet – Environmental or Economic Issue? 41
13 Unfair Forfeiture Law Changed..45
14 Gypsy Moths and the Law..48
15 Legal Medical Cannabis – the First Step.................................51
16 Government Sponsored Prayer is Now Legal 55
17 Same-Sex Marriage Comes to Minnesota 59
18 Kathy and Val: Happily Married at Last 62
19 Fond du Lac Band to swap land..65
20 Green Funerals are now an Option 68

Lake County deals with social ills
21 Violence Against Women (and Men) in Lake County............73
22 The Victim/Witness Coordinator is Here to Help You 76
23 Bobbi and the Safe Harbor Law...79
24 Are there Homeless People Here?...82

Court Procedures in Lake County

25 Lake County Court is eFiling Pioneer 87
26 Rules for OFP Hearings are changed...................................90
27 Can I get a Harassment Restraining Order?...........................93
28 How Should We Choose Judges? 97
29 U.S. Supreme Court as Liberal as People Think 100
30 Nolan Wants to "Restore Democracy"..................................103

FASCINATING NORTH SHORE CASES

Dr. Lynn Rogers and friends

Ely is in St. Louis County, but for people in northern Lake County, it's their "big city" next door. It is the home of two nationally known tourist attractions, the International Wolf Center and the North American Bear Center. The latter was founded in 2007 by Dr. Lynn Rogers, known throughout the world for his research on bears. I read about him in Charlie Russell's book about the brown bears of Kamchatka. But here at home, the Minnesota Department of Natural Resources has decided to close down his research – it's dangerous to humans, they say. So far the lower courts have decided in favor of the DNR but I'm hoping that the appellate courts will rule for Dr. Rogers.

THE MAN WHO WALKS WITH BEARS

A trial that recently took place in St. Paul provided a fascinating look at Dr. Lynn Rogers of Ely, the "man who walks with bears."

Lynn Rogers, age 75, has been studying black bears for almost 50 years. He began as a Ph.D. student at the University of Minnesota. Since then he has radio-tracked over 100 bears in northeastern Minnesota, learning about their socialization, idiosyncrasies, ecological relationships, and death. His work has been compared to that of chimpanzee researcher Jane Goodall. He conducts his studies through an organization known as Wildlife Research Institute, and in 2007 he opened the North American Bear Center in Ely. There have been 13 documentaries about his work made by BBC since 2008, which have been viewed by over 100 million people on Animal Planet, National Geographic, PBS, and the Discovery Channel. More than 500 schools have viewed his den videos.

Since 1999 the Minnesota Department of Natural Resources (DNR) has given annual permits to Dr. Rogers allowing him to place radio collars on a certain number of bears, and to place video cameras at the entrance of bear dens. He places the radio collars without trapping the bears or using tranquilizers. He does this by establishing a trusting relationship with a bear, distracting the bear, and then slipping a collar around its neck.

However, last June the DNR notified Rogers that his research permit was cancelled. They gave three reasons: he has not published scholarly articles about his research; his habituation of bears by hand feeding them creates a public safety issue; and he has behaved unprofessionally with the research bears, they say.

At the trial, the DNR called witnesses who stated that Dr. Rogers' practice of hand-feeding wild bears is "a terrible idea" that is "very dangerous" and increases the risk of bear attacks on the general public. However, the attorney for Dr. Rogers, David Marshall, called witnesses to establish that black bears are usually not aggressive; they may bluff charge, huff, paw the ground, and pop their jaws, but attacks on humans are very rare.

Under Minnesota law, Marshall says, Dr. Rogers needs a permit to radio collar bears only if he has "possession" of the bears he collars. He concedes that traditional methods of collaring wild animals – using drugs or restraints – would constitute exercising possession and control over the animal and thus require a permit. But since Rogers does not use tranquilizers, pens, or traps, he should be able to continue collaring bears and filming them even without a permit, says the attorney. The fact that he feeds the bears, names them, and develops relationships with them as though they were pets, does not mean that he "possesses" them.

Even if a permit were required, the attorney argues that the DNR had no valid reason or "cause" to deny or revoke Dr. Rogers' permit. They relied, he says, on incidents that occurred prior to the most recent issuance of a permit but which they knew about. For example, Rogers used to permit visitors to hand feed the bears, but in 2012 the DNR told him that only he and his assistants could do so, and he has complied with that restriction.

As for scholarly articles, Dr. Rogers says he submitted two articles for publication in 2012; one of these was published in the Journal of Veterinary Diagnostic Investigations and the other was accepted for publication in the journal Ethology. He provided a list of numerous peer-reviewed papers he has published and many talks he has given in the last 15 years. Expert witnesses described Rogers' work as "top-flight research."

The judge who presided at the trial was Tammy L. Pust, who is the Chief Administrative Law Judge at the Minnesota Office of Administrative Hearings. She issued her decision siding with the DNR, which confirmed her ruling in late 2014. Dr. Rogers cannot continue radio-collaring and videotaping wild black bears in northern Minnesota, they said – it's too dangerous to humans. He plans to appeal.

Tim Scannell

Everyone on the North Shore was shocked when the Cook County Attorney in Grand Marais, Tim Scannell, was charged by a grand jury with Criminal Sexual Conduct. He had just won a case against a man charged with the same crime, who returned to court with a gun and shot the prosecutor four times. Suffering from PTSD, Scannell said he "sought solace" in the arms of the 17-year-old family friend for whom he'd once been considered a positive mentor, according to the Duluth News Tribune report of his sentencing. Although there were serious legal questions as to whether his conduct was simply foolish or also criminal, the jury convicted him and the judge sentenced him to jail. I think there a good chance that the Court of Appeals will throw out the conviction.

2

THE CASE AGAINST COUNTY ATTORNEY TIM SCANNELL

It was a shock to everyone last fall when the County Attorney for Cook County, Tim Scannell, was indicted by a grand jury in Duluth for criminal sexual conduct. The indictment charged that he had "sexual contact" with a 16 or 17 year old girl on two occasions in August, 2012. Under Minnesota law the age of consent for sexual relations in 16, but it was alleged that Scannell's acts were a felony because he had a "significant relationship" with the girl and was more than 4 years older than she was; the girl's consent is no defense in such a case.

The term "sexual contact" is defined by Minnesota law as "the intentional touching by the actor of the complainant's intimate parts, or the touching of the clothing covering the immediate area of the intimate parts." According to the search warrant in this case, it is alleged that Scannell and the girl kissed and held hands and that he "touched her chest." Nothing more than that, apparently.

As for the "significant relationship," Minnesota law defines that as the child's parent, stepparent, guardian, other close relative, or an adult who resides with her. Clearly, that doesn't apply to Scannell. His attorney therefore filed a motion to dismiss the charges. The special prosecutor, Tom Heffelfinger, then moved to amend the indictment to change the words "significant relationship" to "in a position of authority" over the girl.

Minnesota law defines "position of authority" as a person who is "charged with any of a parent's rights, duties or responsibilities to a child, or a person who is charged with any duty or responsibility for the health, welfare, or supervision of a child," including a psychotherapist. The search warrant alleges that Scannell was a "family friend, coach, mentor and volunteer," gave her guitar lessons, and "had significant influence over [the girl] and was in a position of power and authority based on his position as county attorney." Nothing more than that, apparently.

The search warrants obtained by the police allowed them to search Tim Scannell's telephone, his computer, and his accounts in Google, Facebook, iCloud, and LinkedIn.

The motion to dismiss and the motion to amend were heard by District Judge Shaun Floerke in Duluth. A week later he denied Scannell's motion to dismiss and granted the prosecutor's motion to amend the indictment. His legal reasoning makes interesting reading. The Minnesota Rules of Criminal Procedure allow the prosecutor to amend an indictment at any time before verdict as long as no additional or different offense is charged. However, this rule only applies after the trial has commenced. Another rule allows the prosecutor to amend criminal complaints at any time, but this does not apply to grand jury indictments since this "would not protect the function of a grand jury." What to do? Judge Floerke decided to allow the amendment anyway, since the amendment "does not prejudice Defendant's substantial rights." Mr. Heffelfinger submitted an affidavit saying that the grand jury "analyzed only the elements" of "position of authority," and "did not consider whether or not Defendant had a significant relationship." Therefore, the judge ruled, the amendment "preserves the grand jury's decision."

Scannell's attorney also asked that all judges in the Sixth Judicial District be removed from the case based on the "politically and emotionally charged status of this matter." He asserted that any judge subject to election could be swayed by community pressure, and asked that a retired judge, not subject to election, be assigned to the case. Judge Floerke also denied this motion, saying that this is not the first criminal case in Minnesota "in which community members have strong feelings about the outcome or which involves elected officials." He went on to say that "the Minnesota Constitution requires that judges in this state are elected. Appointing a retired judge to hear a case simply because there are strong community opinions about it could be seen as unconstitutional."

The trial was held in Duluth and the jury returned a verdict of "guilty." Scannell was sentenced to 30 days in jail and 10 years probation, plus 300 hours of community service. In addition, he must register as a predatory sex offender for ten years. According to the Duluth News Tribune, at his sentencing his lawyer argued that Scannell "wasn't thinking correctly and that PTSD impaired his judgment." Scannell stated "I didn't fully recognize the damage and harm I caused (the victim) until she was on the (witness) stand ... I will never forgive myself for burdening her and her family with my pain."

Dr. Kenneth Petersen

A border patrol agent accidently struck and killed a man who was removing a tree that had fallen across the Gunflint Trail in Cook County. After lots of legal skirmishing, the agent pled guilty to "failure to drive with due care," a misdemeanor. Seems to me it was a pretty light punishment for the agent's negligence. But apparently there were some positive results of this high profile case.

3

DEATH AND A BLACK BOX ON THE GUNFLINT TRAIL

If you go to the webpage for the Lake County District Court, you will find a link for "High Profile Cases" (http://www.mncourts.gov/district/6/?page=210). One of those cases is actually a Cook County case, State of Minnesota v. Maranda Weber. What made that case so famous?

It happened Halloween night in 2007. Dr. Kenneth Petersen, age 67, was on his way home on the Gunflint Trail from a church choir rehearsal. A tree had fallen across the road, so he stopped to cut it up with his chain saw. The high beam lights of his car were aimed at the tree and the hazard lights were on. Another choir member's car was parked behind him as they worked to clear the tree. A border patrol agent named Maranda Weber, age 27, was traveling south and didn't see the tree or the people. Her car struck Petersen at about 50 miles per hour, knocked him into his own vehicle, and he died as a result of his injuries.

Tim Scannell, the County Attorney, considered charging Maranda Weber with felony criminal vehicular homicide, careless driving, and failure to drive with due care. However, the Grand Jury decided to charge only the latter two crimes, both misdemeanors. According to the Minneapolis Star Tribune, many local residents were outraged over the accident. The Border Patrol office in Grand Marais had grown from two agents to about 15 since 2001, and some locals thought they drove carelessly and were unfriendly – "X-File" stuff, as they put it. Scannell said the Border Patrol refused to provide information he requested.

Sheriff Mark Falk said they seem to have "all these big secrets. There seems to be a lack of public accountability."

However, the car Weber was driving had a "black box" installed, which recorded key readings in the seconds before impact. Scannell said it showed that the car did not swerve, brake, or slow before hitting the tree and Dr. Petersen.

Maranda Weber's attorney then went to Federal Court and tried to stop the Cook County proceedings, arguing that she was immune from prosecution in state court because she was on duty at the time, and could not get fair treatment in Cook County. Federal Judge John Tunheim rejected that claim in late December, 2008. In June, 2009, Judge Kenneth Sandvik rejected Weber's motion to dismiss the Cook County charges. The case was finally resolved in November, 2009, when Weber pled guilty to failure to drive with due care. She was sentenced to pay a fine of $200 plus costs of $90, turning the crime into a petty misdemeanor.

According to Dr. Petersen's obituary in the Duluth News Tribune, he had worked with Native American children in Alaska for 34 years, serving as chief of pediatrics and chief of epidemiology in Anchorage. He worked with another physician, Dr. Rob Burgess, who became his life partner for 31 years (they could not marry at that time, of course). He was a dedicated Lutheran. At Weber's sentencing, Dr. Burgess had this to say: "We have to look at finding out what happened and work to prevent it from happening again ... Border Patrol agents have been acting like adversaries, when we should be working together." To Maranda Weber he said "I knew Ken, and I know that he would forgive you."

Judge Kenneth Sandvik also expressed his opinion about the Border Patrol at the sentencing, saying that concerns regarding their handling of the matter were justified. Relations between the agency and the community have been too adversarial, he said. "The Border Patrol can learn to treat their community ... as though they are part of that community."

What has happened since these events occurred? According to Cook County Sheriff Mark Falk, attitudes have greatly improved since then, and local law enforcement now has "excellent relations" with the Border Patrol. He believes that the Border Patrol now has a "positive image in the community." Molly Hicken, the acting Cook County attorney, told me that she agrees with this assessment, and says that Border Patrol agents have become more involved with the community of Grand Marais. Michael Pauley, the Supervisory Agent at the Border Patrol, told me that he also agrees that relations have improved since the Weber case. However, he would not speculate as to the cause of the improvement in relations. His boss, Richard Fortunato, would not comment and referred me to the Border Patrol's Office of Public Affairs in Detroit. That office did not return my phone call.

James Manahan in front of Spur Station

Condemnation cases don't usually get much publicity. But the Spur gas station, sitting on a hill at the entrance to Silver Bay, is an eyesore that every traveler on Highway 61 notices. It sits there year after year, out of business and ugly. The owners said it was "taken" from them by the Minnesota Highway Department, since changes in the highway made it impossible to stay in business. The State of Minnesota denied that there had been a condemnation of the property. After years of litigation, Judge Michael Cuzzo ruled that it was indeed a "taking," and a jury awarded damages of $812,000. Later the judge awarded the owners additional compensation for interest and attorney fees. It's always gratifying when average citizens can win a case against the government!

4

THE SILVER BAY SPUR STATION CONDEMNATION CASE

When they bought the old Amoco station in Silver Bay, it seemed like an ideal location. Right on the corner of Outer Drive (the main entrance into town) and Highway 61 (the only highway along the North Shore). The buyers (Donna Knaffla McCurdy, Bobbi Boman, and Danny Knaffla) changed it to a Spur station and got off to a good start in 2002.

Then in 2006 the State of Minnesota Department of Transportation (MnDOT) did some construction to improve Highway 61. They built a divider separating north-bound and south-bound traffic. They closed highway access to the Spur station. They built a new access road a couple of blocks north of the station. They installed a curb in the center of the entrance from Outer Drive, resulting in two smaller entry-ways. Now larger vehicles (RVs, trucks, vehicles towing a boat or camper) can't turn around and exit onto Outer Drive, and no one can exit directly onto Highway 61.

At first the folks in Silver Bay showed support for the owners and sales went up slightly. But tourists as well as locals eventually stopped patronizing the place and sales went down. And down. And eventually the station closed.

The owners hired a lawyer and sued MnDOT. They claimed that their property had been "taken" since it could no longer be used as a gas station, and they asked for compensation. The judge in Two Harbors agreed in 2009 that there had been a "taking" and ordered MnDOT to begin a condemnation action so the amount of damages could be determined.

One of the issues in the case was whether the taking by the State has forced the owners to relocate in order to continue in business. If so, they are entitled under Minnesota law to damages <u>at a minimum</u> sufficient to buy a comparable property. MnDOT argued that relocation wasn't mandatory, so the Minnesota law doesn't apply.

At the trial, the testimony showed that the new access road was difficult to use, especially by large vehicles. It is narrow and has two 90 degree turns. The DOT refuses to plow or maintain the access road. There is no left turn lane for north-bound vehicles, which creates a traffic hazard. There are no signs at the entry to the access road. There is not even a written agreement allowing the owners to continue using this access, which is actually on land owned by North Shore Mining Company.

The testimony also showed that trucks delivering fuel to the station now have difficulty using the access road, often getting stuck in the snow, and being at risk of losing control because of the incline and 90 degree turns. The owners testified that, because of loss of tourism traffic and loss of revenue, they can no longer operate a gas station and convenience store at that location. Several witnesses testified that the site is no longer suitable for a gas station due to the redesigned access.

Judge Michael Cuzzo issued his decision. He ruled that "it is no longer financially feasible to operate a gas station" on the site, that they "must relocate," and that they are entitled to seek "minimum compensation" sufficient to buy a comparable property. A trial was then held to determine the amount of compensation to which the owners are entitled, and the jury awarded them $830,000, less $18,000 for the remaining value of the land. Eventually the state settled and agreed to pay $750,000. Later Judge Cuzzo awarded the owners additional compensation for interest and attorney fees.

Customers line up at the Last Place on Earth

The Last Place on Earth was the most popular head shop in Minnesota, perhaps in America. On Superior Street in downtown Duluth, you could buy all sorts of "herbal incense" and "bath salts" to get high. There was always a long line of customers outside the front door, and the owner made millions of dollars. He insisted that there was no law prohibiting sale of the substances he sold, but the government argued that they violated the "analogue" law since they were closely related to illegal drugs. The jury agreed with the government; Jim Carlson was convicted and sentenced to 17 years in prison. The government also seized all of his cash and real estate, worth millions, as "proceeds of a crime." Somehow it all seems like an overreaction.

5

THE LAST PLACE ON EARTH IS CLOSED

Everybody seemed happy when Jim Carlson, the head shop guy in Duluth, was convicted. Everybody, that is, except people concerned about the rule of law and constitutional rights. They had some doubts.

Carlson is the owner of The Last Place on Earth in downtown Duluth. He sold such things as "herbal incense" and "bath salts" and "spice," synthetic drugs that are (he thought) legal alternatives to marijuana and cocaine. His store was extremely popular – people lined up outside to buy his products.

In early October the federal jury in Duluth convicted him of 51 felonies. The 12 jurors also convicted Carlson's girlfriend, Lava Haugen, and his son, Joseph Gellerman.

The Mayor of Duluth, Don Ness, was quick to respond. "There is a great sense of relief in the city of Duluth that we won't have this massive problem in our downtown, going forward," he said. An owner of the printing company next to the head shop offered his opinion: "It was like a crack neighborhood."

So who could object to the jury's verdict? The law is clear – you can't sell illegal drugs. Both federal and state laws carefully define controlled substances, putting them in five different schedules according to harmfulness. [Note that heroin, LSD, and marijuana are all together on Schedule I, which is obviously ridiculous.] The lists are constantly getting longer, as new chemical compounds are created. In fact, a former employee testified that Carlson would stop selling any substance that was added to the list of illegal drugs.

According to the testimony, the stuff Carlson was selling isn't on those lists. Some of them have very similar components, but they aren't identical. The prosecution argued that they were "closely related substances," so their sale violated the federal "analogue" law. That law bans substances with similar chemical structures and effects to controlled substances already on the government's official list. The U.S. Attorney said that in some instances in Carlson's case, there was only a single molecule change from substances banned by the Federal Drug Administration, so their sale is also illegal. The jury bought that argument.

Carlson's attorney, Randy Tigue, however, argued that "this is a prosecution by ambush of someone who obeys the law … We do not have secret laws" in this country.

And Joseph Daly, emeritus professor at Hamline Law School in St. Paul, said the synthetic drug law is vague and could lead to a successful appeal. "I think the defense may have a good argument," he told the Minneapolis Star Tribune.

Even beyond the argument that the law is vague and ambiguous, this case raises the question of why we criminalize potentially harmful drugs in the first place. Even if The Last Place on Earth is closed, people who want go get high can always buy drugs (including alcohol) that have that effect. DFL Representative Dan Schoen has been battling so-called "synthetic marijuana," and calls the new designer drugs "a special demon." But he admits that the criminal law won't stop people from buying drugs online. "I'm not going to pretend that we're going to wipe out drugs," he said, "but we're going to make it harder." Given the amount of money we spend on the "War on Drugs," one must ask if this makes any sense.

Protesters march at Baby Veronica hearing

The entire Arrowhead region, including Lake County, is home to many Native Americans, so the case of Baby Veronica was followed closely here. The father and the adoptive parents of the girl fought the case in Oklahoma, South Carolina, and the United States Supreme Court. The courts eventually ruled against the birth father, and Indian families everywhere (as well as fathers) will be negatively affected by their interpretation of the Indian Child Welfare Act.

6

THE SAGA OF BABY VERONICA, NATIVE AMERICAN CHILD

Baby Veronica, whose father is an Indian (a member of the Cherokee Nation), has become famous even though she is only four years old. Her custody battle has been fought in Oklahoma, South Carolina, and the U.S. Supreme Court.

The saga started in 2009 when Veronica's mother, Christina Maldonado, told Veronica's father, Dusten Brown, that she was pregnant. Brown eventually told Maldonado that he relinquished his rights to the unborn child.

The mother then began making arrangements to place the child for adoption with a couple in South Carolina, Matthew and Melanie Capobianco, who are white. Four months after the birth of the child, Brown was served with notice of the proposed adoption. The Indian tribe did not receive any notice. Since Brown was serving with the U.S. Army in Iraq, he got the adoption proceedings delayed.

The case was finally heard in South Carolina in September, 2011. The judge denied the Capobianco's petition to adopt Veronica, and ordered that the child be returned to Brown as the biological father. The ruling was based on the Indian Child Welfare Act (the ICWA), a federal law designed to prevent the separation of Native American children from their biological families and tribes. So Veronica went to live in Oklahoma with her father.

The Capobiancos appealed and the South Carolina Supreme Court also ruled against them. In a 3 to 2 decision the majority ruled that the ICWA allows an Indian to relinquish his rights to a child only if it is in writing, before a judge, and signed at least ten days after the child's birth. The Capobiancos also made no effort to prevent the breakup of the Indian family, as required by the ICWA. Therefore the child would continue to live with her father.

The Capobiancos appealed again, this time to the United States Supreme Court. The Obama administration argued on behalf of Brown, the father, as did 22 "friends of the court." However, on June 25, 2013, the Supreme Court ruled in favor of the Capobiancos. It was a split decision, 5 to 4. The majority (Chief Justice Roberts and Justices Alito, Kennedy, Thomas, and Breyer) decided that the ICWA does not apply to an Indian father who has never had custody of his child, relying on the words "continued custody" in the statute. The judges said that the ICWA does not prevent a non-Indian couple from adopting when no Indian has formally sought to adopt the child.

Justice Sotomayor dissented, along with Justices Ginsburg, Kagan, and Scalia. She wrote that the word "continued" in the statute did not only refer to the past, but also to continued custody in the future. She said that the majority opinion was destroying a father's relationship with a child solely because he did not have custody, which turned the law "upside down," and ignored the very purpose of the ICWA.

So baby Veronica's custody case went back to the South Carolina Supreme Court, which ruled in another 3 to 2 decision that the adoption be finalized and custody returned to the Copobiancos. The majority said "There is absolutely no need to compound any suffering that Baby Girl may experience through continued litigation." The attorney for the Cherokee Nation called this decision "heartbreaking." The Copobiancos said "We look forward to seeing Veronica's smiling face in the coming days and will do everything in our power to make her homecoming as smooth as possible." Eventually the father, Dusten Brown, dropped his efforts to gain custody of Baby Veronica.

Lou's Fish House

What exactly constitutes sexual harassment under the Minnesota Human Rights Act? A case involving the popular smoked fish store in Two Harbors, Lou's Fish House, has helped us understand this term. We now know that victims can sue for damages even if they never suffered any loss of pay and were not fired. The case went all the way to the Minnesota Supreme Court and back to Judge Cuzzo before the women finally won their case. It took a long time, but justice was finally done.

7

DID LOU'S FISH HOUSE BREAK THE LAW?

Three women who worked for Lou's Fish House sued their employer and its owner, Brian Zapolski, claiming that he sexually harassed them in violation of the Minnesota Human Rights Act. The District Court judge in Two Harbors found that Zapolski touched one woman's posterior with his hands on two occasions, showed her and other employees a nude photo in a Playboy magazine, suggested that she watch a pornographic DVD, frequently asked her about her sexual position preferences, described his sexual desires in a "very explicit" manner, sought one employee's assistance in soliciting "other young women to have sex with him," and "bragged to her about his sexual prowess." Zapolski also talked to her about orgasms. All this made the employees feel "violated" and "embarrassed."

The judge nonetheless threw out the case, ruling that this conduct does not violate Minnesota law. The women appealed and the Court of Appeals reversed the decision, holding that the women are entitled to damages as a matter of law.

Then the Minnesota Supreme Court weighed in. It's hard to figure out what their decision means, so you might want to read it yourself:

http://mn.gov/lawlib/archive/supct/1305/OPA112178-0522.pdf

It seems that they agree with the Court of Appeals that the law was broken. The fact that Zapolski directed inappropriate sexual comments at both male and female employees is not relevant, they say, nor is the fact that the employees did not lose pay or other benefits. Nonetheless,

"We are not able to ascertain exactly how [these] errors of law impacted the district court's decision to dismiss the Employees' claims." So they sent the case back to Two Harbors to "reevaluate the evidence using the correct legal standard." Does that mean they have to go through another trial? Or just that the judge has to write another decision based on the evidence at the first trial?

Three Supreme Court justices (Wilhelmina Wright, Alan Page, and Paul Anderson) dissented, saying they could not understand why the case was being sent back to the District Court. Justice Paul Anderson called the refusal to rule "extraordinary," and said this:

> *I believe something more needs to be said about the message the majority delivers to Minnesota's citizens, whether those citizens are male or female, young or old, rich or poor. The unfortunate consequence of the majority's opinion may well be that offensive and repulsive sexual misconduct in the workplace, like Zapolski's verbal and physical misconduct, will be much more difficult to curtail in Minnesota and that many victims of similar misconduct will be left without a remedy under the law.*

After reconsidering the case, Judge Michael Cuzzo ordered the defendants, Two Harbors Fish Co. doing business as Lou's Fish House, and BWZ Enterprises, LLC, to pay the three plaintiffs a total of $312,751.83.

James Manahan at Eveleth iron mine

The first sexual harassment class-action lawsuit in United States history happened on the iron range of northern Minnesota. A book about the case became a movie, <u>North County</u>, one of the most powerful documentaries ever filmed. The plaintiffs eventually settled with the mining company for $3.5 million.

8

SEXUAL HARASSMENT IN NORTH COUNTRY MINES

Writing my column about the Lou's Fish House case reminded me of the movie *North Country*. It came out in 2005 and starred Charlize Theron and Frances McDormand, both of whom were nominated for Academy Awards. The plot involves women who were sexually harassed at the iron mine in Eveleth where they worked. They brought a class action and eventually won substantial money damages. The film was shot mostly in Eveleth, Virginia, and Chisholm.

The movie is based on a book that is based on a true story. The actual court case, *Lois Jenson v. Eveleth Taconite Company*, was the first class-action sexual harassment lawsuit in the United States. It was started in 1984, and took 14 years before it was finally settled.

In 1974, the U.S. Department of Labor and the Equal Employment Opportunity Commission required steel companies to set aside 20% of their jobs for women and minority men. Lois Jenson began working at the Eveleth taconite mine in 1975. After enduring a lot of sexual harassment and abusive language from co-workers, she filed a complaint with the Minnesota Department of Human Rights. The employer, EVTAC, refused to do anything about the situation. An attorney named Paul Sprenger filed Jenson's case in U.S. District Court, and the trial started in December, 1992. Judge Richard Kyle ruled that the company should have prevented the misconduct, and set another trial to determine the amount of damages to be paid to the women. Patrick McNulty of Duluth was appointed to hear this part of the case, and the trial lasted for several months in 1995. McNulty awarded the women $11,000 each, a surprisingly low amount; he concluded that the women were "paranoid" and "puritanical." The women appealed and the award was reversed by the 8th Circuit Court of Appeals. In 1998, just before the new trial was to begin, the fifteen women settled and Eveleth Mines agreed to pay them a total of $3.5 million. (More facts about the case can be found in Wikipedia. org at http://en.wikipedia.org/wiki/Jenson_v._Eveleth_Taconite_Co.)

This case was extremely important because it was the first class-action lawsuit for sexual harassment. Prior to this, victims (men or women) had to sue individually, and the expenses of such protracted litigation made it economically impossible to mount a strong challenge to the wealthy employers.

The book that describes the case is called *Class Action: The Story of Lois Jenson and the Landmark Case That Changed Sexual Harassment Law* by Clara Bingham and Laura Leedy Gansler (Doubleday Press, 2002). Used copies can now be bought for one cent at Amazon.com! Like the Erin Brockovich case, this Northern Minnesota case is the basis for both an important legal precedent and a great movie.

LOCAL LEGAL LEGENDS

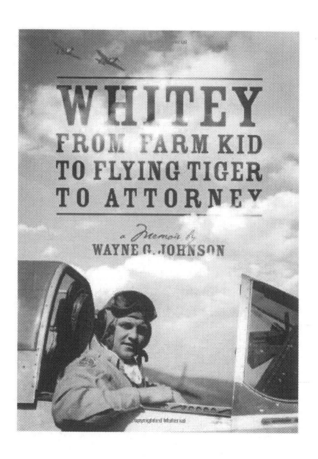

When I first came to Lake County, Minnesota, I made sure to look up Wayne Johnson. Known as Whitey, he is the longest serving City Attorney in U.S history – 53 years in Silver Bay. He's also famous for his role in the Reserve Mining Case, the longest and most complex environmental case in history. He tells some wonderful stories in his autobiography, *Whitey* (Langdon Street Press, Minneapolis, 2011).

9

FLYING TIGER WHITEY: LONGEST SERVING CITY ATTORNEY IN US HISTORY

One of Minnesota's top lawyers lives in Lake County. Wayne Johnson, known to his friends as Whitey, has written his autobiography, a "must-read" book for anyone who wants to know the history of this county. It is called "Whitey – from Farm Kid to Flying Tiger to Attorney" (Langdon Street Press, Minneapolis, 2011).

An accomplished story teller, Johnson fills his 454 page book with wonderful anecdotes about his childhood on a farm and his Word War II years as a fighter pilot in China. But the best part of the book is his stories about practicing law in Lake County.

After opening his law office in Beaver Bay in 1952, he became City Attorney the next year. In 1956 he became City Attorney for the new village of Silver Bay. When he retired in 2009 he had set a record as the longest-serving city attorney in the history of the United States.

Johnson also handled civil and criminal cases on behalf of local clients. They ranged from a negligent fire claim against Standard Oil Company, to the defense of a man accused of murder in Cook County, to a suit against a hospital, to a claim by a farmer who was terribly burned after a propane tank exploded.

The most interesting litigation, however, involved Reserve Mining Company. For almost 16 years Johnson represented the cities of Beaver Bay and Silver Bay as well as many other cities and counties in the longest and most complex environmental case in history. Johnson's job was to prove that the dumping of "tailings" into Lake Superior did not constitute a health hazard.

Johnson was in court constantly, from Duluth to Minneapolis to St. Louis to the U.S. Supreme Court. He says he spent some 3,000 hours a year on this one case! When he felt that Judge Miles Lord had ceased to be impartial, he convinced the Court of Appeals to take Lord off the case and substitute Judge Edward Devitt, an almost unprecedented achievement. Finally the courts ruled that there was not sufficient evidence to establish that Reserve's operation constituted a health hazard.

Reserve Mining had to find $450,000,000 to build a tailings deposit area called Mile Post 7, so Johnson got the city of Silver Bay to raise that amount through revenue bonds. When the company later went bankrupt, the bonds became worthless and the people who bought them took a total loss. Since Johnson had insisted that the bonds be revenue bonds rather than the typical government issued bonds, the city did not take a loss.

There are many more fascinating stories in the book. About building the Silver Bay airport, now known as the Wayne Johnson Silver Bay Airport. About being named "Mr. Aviation of Minnesota" in 1968, and being named to the Minnesota Aviation Hall of Fame in 2001. About losing his legs to gangrene when he was 87 years of age.

Whitey is now 93 years of age and still living in Beaver Bay with his wife of more than 50 years, Delores. He says he feels good and has learned to get around "pretty well" on his prosthetic legs. And if you get a chance to visit him, he still has many more interesting stories he can tell you about the practice of law in Lake County during the last 62 years.

Judge Michael Cuzzo with his son Alex

Judge Michael Cuzzo has been the judge in Lake and Cook Counties – part of the Arrowhead Region – since 2011. Most judges in Minnesota were appointed by the governor, but Cuzzo won the job the old fashioned way, winning a hotly contested election in November 2010. Although he was a "Super Lawyer" in Duluth, he was not well known in Lake County, but the voters of St. Louis and Carlton Counties put him over the top. Since then he has become a popular and highly respected judge.

10

DULUTH SUPER-LAWYER JUDGE

In November, 2010, Michael Cuzzo was elected district court judge in the 6th Judicial District. The 6th District covers the Arrowhead region of Minnesota – Cook, Lake, St. Louis, and Carlton Counties. A majority of the voters (61%) in Cook County and Lake County voted for the other candidate, Tim Costley. But Cuzzo got over 60% of the votes throughout the district, and won the election. Now he is the trial court judge assigned to Cook County and Lake County. Who is he?

Michael Cuzzo grew up in Duluth, and graduated from Denfeld High School and UMD (1980). He then attended the U of M Law School and graduated with honors in 1983.

During his career as a lawyer, Cuzzo represented injured people. He was president of the Duluth Trial Lawyers Association and a member of Minnesota Association for Justice. He was selected as a "Super Lawyer" every year since 2003, and in 2009 he was named by Minnesota Law & Politics magazine as one of the state's Top 40 workers' compensation lawyers.

During his years practicing law, Cuzzo was active in numerous community activities. He was on the board of the YMCA, the Family of God Lutheran Church, and the Duluth Community Chaplaincy. He also served as a coach and a judge for high school and college Mock Trials.

Being what he calls a "pretty good fisherman," Judge Cuzzo spends a lot of time (with wife Diana and son Alex) at their cabin on the Caribou trail. He says he likes hunting, camping, and "anything outdoors." He also likes getting up early. When I interviewed him early one morning, he had already been at his office in Two Harbors since 6:30 a.m. Besides judging cases, he meets often with social workers, probation officers, and others to improve justice for children and child protection services. He also gets prosecutors and defense attorneys together for lunch to discuss improvements in handling criminal cases.

When Cuzzo ran for judge in 2010, he said this: "The question of how someone is treated in my court will not be one of color, status, culture, or connections. Decisions will be based upon the law, facts, and individual circumstances surrounding each case. I have been proud to represent people with diverse backgrounds, and will continue to treat all with respect."

I asked him how he gets along with the seven lawyers who ran against him in the 2010 primary election (he came in first with 36% of the vote). He replied that he works well with all of them, and they treat each other with mutual respect. In fact, he says his door is open to everyone in the courthouse – "I will listen to groups that have suggestions to offer on how to improve the justice system, including the juvenile justice system."

So if you have any suggestions, drop Judge Cuzzo a line at Lake County Courthouse, 601 Third Ave., Two Harbors, MN 55616.

Mitch Costley (L) and Tim Costley (R)

The busiest law firm in Lake County is the Costleys, father and son. Mitch has been practicing since 1967, and Tim since 2000. If you look at the court calendar, you will see one or both of their names listed often, handling contract disputes, divorces, criminal cases, and just about anything else. They also never shy away from taking controversial stands on political issues in the county.

11

LIKE FATHER, LIKE SON ON
THE NORTH SHORE

The only father/son law firm on the North Shore, and one of the few such in Minnesota, is Costley Law Firm of Two Harbors.

The Dad, Mitch Costley, is a descendent of pioneers who came here before Minnesota was a state. He grew up in Two Harbors and has practiced law here since 1967. He became City Attorney for Two Harbors a year later, and in 1971 he was elected Lake County Attorney. He resigned after being re-elected, in order to devote himself to running his law firm – and raising four kids. Later he was a part-time public defender for about 20 years, representing criminal defendants who could not afford a lawyer. He has also served on the Lake County Historical Society Board for the last eight years, and was Chair of the Lake County Housing & Redevelopment Authority for almost 30 years. However, his proudest achievement, he told me, was being the second person in Lake County history to become an Eagle Scout.

Tim Costley has practiced law with his Dad since 2000. He has also been active in community affairs, serving on the Board of Supervisors of Alden Township for several years, Chair of Ducks Unlimited, and a board member of the Chamber of Commerce. Like his father, he has represented people who couldn't afford a lawyer, as a member of the Northeast Minnesota Volunteer Attorney program.

Mitch actually discouraged his son from going to law school. "Being a lawyer," he said, "is too much work." But now he admits that he loves practicing law with his son. "It's the most enjoyable experience I could have had," he says. The two of them do many things together besides handling lawsuits (such as fishing). The secret to working together successfully, he says, is having a good relationship, which Mitch and Tim have had since Tim's childhood.

In 2010 Tim ran for district court judge, and now says that he doesn't regret it. However, trying to get elected in the 6th Judicial District (Carlton, Cook, Lake, and St. Louis Counties), when you aren't well known in the larger counties, was not a lot of fun, he says. Both he and Mitch support the Impartial Justice Act, which would allow judges to be appointed based on merit, subject to recall for failure to perform their duties. This bi-partisan proposal of former Governor Al Quie was supposed to be on the ballot this fall as a constitutional amendment, but failed to clear legislative hurdles.

Mitch and Tim Costley have also spoken out in opposition to the attempt to make the Lake County Auditor/Treasurer and Recorder appointed positions. In fact, they drafted a petition opposing the change and got enough signatures to put that question on the ballot. Although only 721 signatures were required (10% of registered voters), almost 1,400 voters signed the petition. The proposed change (to appoint instead of elect) would "take away a hard-won American right to vote," Mitch said. "We're a high voter turnout county and people take their right to vote seriously. I don't care how you vote. I just want you to be able to vote on it."

And his son, Tim, added "I think there are a lot of people that are mad about a lot of things that have been going on in the county. I think this is the one way now they can finally show that they're not happy." On November 4, 2014, Lake County voters cast their ballots and let the world know they agree with Mitch and Tim Costley on this issue.

Big Legal Changes Affecting the North Shore

There's a lot of passion about copper mining in northern Minnesota. Opponents call it "sulfide mining" and say that extracting copper releases sulfuric acid that will pollute our water for centuries. Supporters say that the world needs copper, it can be mined ecologically, and it will create lots of jobs. It seems to me that the copper is going to be extracted someday, and our job is to make sure it is done with a minimum of environmental damage. The battle is still being waged.

POLYMET – ENVIRONMENTAL
OR ECONOMIC ISSUE?

"Mining supports us, we support mining." "Protect our air and our water – stop PolyMet!" What is the truth about the big mining controversy along the western edge of Lake County?

We were able to read the latest Environmental Impact Statement (SDEIS) and submit comments to the agencies in charge of the approval process (MN Department of Natural Resources, U.S. Forest Service, and U.S. Army Corps of Engineers). You can find the SDEIS at http://www.dnr.state.mn.us/input/environmentalreview/polymet/index.html. Here are some of the facts:

PolyMet Mining, Inc. (a company headquartered in Toronto, Canada) proposes to create an open pit copper, nickel, cobalt and precious metals mine near Babbitt, MN. They plan to transport the minerals 7 miles by rail to Hoyt Lakes and process them in the old LTV Steel plant. Neither the proposed mine nor the processing facility is in the watershed containing the Boundary Waters Canoe Area Wilderness. They also want to exchange 6722 acres of land they own inside Superior National Forest for 6650 acres of forest land at Babbitt where the minerals have been discovered.

According to the SDEIS, the mining operations would last about 20 years. They expect to remove 533,000,000 tons of ore and waste rock from the deposit. When the minerals are exhausted, PolyMet says they will remove the infrastructure and will treat the water in the area for "as long as required in meeting water quality standards." They also promise that "financial protections would remain in place until the site is maintenance free, including water treatment." They are guessing that this means 200 years at the mine site and 500 years at the processing plant. PolyMet has not yet given any details of how they would guarantee compliance with their promises.

Many people are excited about the favorable economic impact this project would have in our part of the state. Others are more concerned about possible environmental destruction. Here is what the SDEIS says about these concerns:

1. Water quality – Sulfate and metals could be released, that would affect living things in the water for many years. Aluminum and lead would increase in waters north of the Embarrass River watershed. PolyMet promises to use reverse osmosis to treat the water for sulfate, liner systems to catch rain that falls on the waste rock stockpiles, and a cap for the tailings basin. They also say that this will alleviate concerns about the effect of sulfate on wild rice production.

2. Water quantity – If water from the tailings basin pond is not sufficient, they will take water from Colby Lake, which they estimate will be an average of 275 gallons per minute. They plan to capture 90% of the groundwater seepage at the tailings basin, and after being treated the water would be discharged into the Partridge and Embarrass Rivers.

3. Air quality – The project would emit air pollutants such as sulfur dioxide, nitrogen oxides, greenhouse gases, and dust. PolyMet has proposed state-of-the-art controls to limit emissions, including air filters during rock crushing.

4. Cultural Resources – The project would affect historic and cultural resources important to the Ojibwe people, including the Bois Forte, Fond du Lac, and Grand Portage Bands of Chippewa, by excavation, filling, and earth-moving that could result in visual obstructions, noise, vibration, and dust. Cultural resources include the Laurentian Divide (regarded as a sacred place to the Ojibwe people), and part of the Beaver Bay to Lake Vermillion Trail. PolyMet says they will minimize effects by moving activities away from such resources.

5. Endangered Species – Some protected species, such as Canada lynx and gray wolf, would be affected by noise, vibration, and

human traffic. Habitat could be removed or destroyed, and changes in water quality could affect animals, including bald eagles, wood turtles, voles, and tiger beetles. PolyMet will restore certain lands when they leave, and "this could potentially create new habitat, though the process could take decades."

Ron Meador, a journalist and former director of Friends of the Boundary Waters Wilderness, wrote a surprisingly favorable article on this issue in MinnPost. He said that no permits for sulfide mining should be given unless PolyMet can demonstrate proven ability to operate and close down their operations without lasting environmental harm, and back up their promises with ironclad financial guarantees to protect taxpayers. And then he said that he thinks PolyMet might do so! He is "highly impressed with the technological advances that seem to be within their reach … I'm willing to be persuaded that newer mining technologies and stronger environmental commitments could make the PolyMet project a dramatic departure from hard-rock mining's terrible history of lasting harm in this country and others." For additional thoughts on financial assurances see State Auditor Rebecca Otto's column at http://www.startribune.com/opinion/commentaries/232745641.html

I WANT YOUR

MONEY, JEWELRY, CAR, BOAT AND HOUSE.

It makes sense to seize a criminal's assets if they are the profits of criminal activity, as in the case of the Duluth head shop (p. 17). But sometimes the government can be over-zealous, and in some cases property was forfeited even if the defendant was never convicted of a crime. That unjust situation has now been corrected by the Minnesota legislature and governor.

13

UNFAIR FORFEITURE LAW CHANGED

A couple of years ago the Two Harbors Police Department found the money to buy a video surveillance system to be installed in key areas around town. The department reported that it would be better able to keep an eye on places like the breakwater, the band shell, and the skate park where there have been incidences of vandalism. The equipment was purchased with drug forfeiture funds received by the department.

The Lake County Sheriff's office has also benefitted from the forfeiture law. They were able to buy new pistols for the Sheriff, Undersheriff and 14 deputies, and to buy upgraded shotguns for the squad cars.

What most people didn't know was that police and sheriffs in Minnesota could keep property, vehicles, and cash seized in drug cases or drive-by shootings regardless of the outcome of the criminal case. If a suspect was found not guilty, they could still lose their property in civil court unless they could prove it was not involved in a crime.

Specifically, Minnesota law (like that of most states) required a person to bring a civil suit within 60 days following seizure of his or her property. As the plaintiff, he or she had the burden of proving a negative – that the property was not involved in a crime. Because of this, and the cost of litigation, more than 95% of those charged with a drug crime in Minnesota did not file a civil case to get back their property.

This has been profitable for law enforcement agencies. A report by the Institute for Justice found that forfeiture revenue in Minnesota grew by 75% from 2003 to 2010, earning police almost $30 million. In 2012 alone, there were 6,851 property seizures worth a collective $6.7 million.

In one case in Massachusetts the federal government threatened civil forfeiture against a motel owner, Russ Caswell, because of 15 drug arrests at his motel. He was never charged with a crime, but the government argued that he was "facilitating" drug crimes. As he wrote in The Washington Times, "Over a 14-year period I rented out rooms to almost 200,000 guests. The government only offered as evidence 15 drug arrests. Not 15,000 or 1,500 – just 15. [Bigger motels] down the road had more drug activity than my motel." Eventually he won his case. http://www.ij.org/massachusetts-civil-forfeiture

The forfeiture law in Minnesota was famously abused by the Metro Gang Strike Force, which has now been disbanded. However, they had to pay $840,000 in settlements to victims who had their property illegally seized.

Now the Minnesota statutes have been changed, effective for crimes committed on or after August 1, 2014. The new law requires the police to return the seized property if there is no criminal conviction. The bill faced stiff opposition from law enforcement agencies, but in March the Star Tribune called it an "outrage" that lawmakers were "dragging their feet on one of the big common-sense changes" to the state's forfeiture laws. The bill was backed by the American Civil Liberties Union and the Institute for Justice. Eventually the bill passed the state senate 55 to 5 and the state house 120 to 0. It was signed into law by Gov. Mark Dayton in May.

There is one exception in the new law. A person who is not charged with a drug crime because he or she agrees to provide information regarding the criminal activity of another person can still lose their property, even without a conviction. Further, if a defendant receives a stay of adjudication or is referred to a diversion program, it is still considered a conviction for purposes of the forfeiture law.

Here in Lake County, the new law won't cause much of a change. Both Sheriff Carey Johnson and Two Harbors Chief of Police Kevin Ruberg told me that they typically have waited for a conviction before going through with a forfeiture. "It seems like the fairest way to treat people," said Ruberg.

Gypsy Moth egg mass

Gypsy Moth laying eggs

Who would have guessed that it would be illegal to carry moths out of Lake County? The Minnesota Department of Agriculture has issued a regulation, specific to Lake County and Cook County, requiring everyone leaving those counties to first check their vehicle and equipment for gypsy moths. Does the government have the right to do that?

14

GYPSY MOTHS AND THE LAW

We residents of Lake County and Cook County are subject to a new law that applies only to us. As of July 1, 2014, we have to check for gypsy moths (plus their caterpillars, eggs, and pupae).

The Minnesota Department of Agriculture has given us a checklist of items we have to examine before we move them to another county or state. There are 88 items on the list, including camping equipment, boats, RVs, firewood, trash cans, flagpoles, lawnmowers, bikes, sleds, cars – you can read the whole list (with pictures of moth egg masses) at

http://www.hungrypests.com/YourMoveGypsyMothFree/pdf/Gypsy-Moth-Brochure.pdf

And it's not only residents – visitors to our two counties are required to do the same thing before leaving. Also loggers have to check their trucks and loads to make sure they aren't transporting moth eggs out of Lake and Cook Counties.

What happens if you fail to check? You are subject to a fine of up to $7,500 and/or 90 days in jail. The Duluth News Tribune reported, however, that a spokesman for the Department of Agriculture said "we are not going to have inspectors standing along Highway 61 to enforce this for everyone who drives by in a camper." So compliance, for the time being anyway, will apparently be voluntary and we will be on the honor system.

What gives the Department of Agriculture the right to impose these requirements on us? It turns out there is a Minnesota statute,

Section 18G.06, that gives the Commissioner of Agriculture the power to impose quarantines. The law says "The commissioner may impose a quarantine restricting or regulating the production, <u>movement</u>, or existence of plants, plant products, agricultural commodities, crop seed, farm products, <u>or other articles or materials</u> in order that the introduction or <u>spread of a plant pest may be prevented or limited</u> or an existing plant pest may be controlled or eradicated." The phrase "other articles or materials" apparently means the 88 items on the list. This is the first time the commissioner has imposed a quarantine of gypsy moths; he believes that the threat gives him no other choice.

Gypsy moths eat leaves, especially aspen, birch, willow, poplar, and oak. They can defoliate vast areas quickly, causing already stressed trees to die. Last summer the state trapped more than 71,000 gypsy moths along and near the North Shore – a record number. According to the Duluth News Tribune, pest experts have sprayed "just about every inch of Lake and Cook counties from 2006-2011" in an effort to slow the advancement of the moth. But that effort has now ended, moving west into St. Louis and Carlton counties. Officials expect the first major forest defoliation in Lake and Cook counties within 3 to 5 years.

The first gypsy moth quarantines were enacted in 1912 in New England. Minnesota is the 22nd state to be completely or partially quarantined for this invasive species. The U.S. Department of Agriculture has now issued an interstate commerce quarantine that parallels the Minnesota quarantine.

Here is what the U.S.D.A. says you have to do before taking any of the 88 items out of Lake and Cook counties: "Carefully inspect all surfaces and crevices of your outdoor household articles for gypsy moth egg masses. Remove and destroy any egg masses you find. Scrape them off with a putty knife, stiff brush, or similar hand tool. Dispose of egg masses and other life stages in a container of hot, soapy water, or place them in a plastic bag, seal it, and set it in the sun."

So any of us who want to help stop the spread of gypsy moths should follow the new rules if we take the listed items out of Lake and Cook counties. In fact, we might be stopped at the border if we take these items into Canada. Even without the threat of a fine or jail, it seems like a good idea to do what we can to save our trees and forests.

Legalization of marijuana is a hot topic now everywhere in America. In Minnesota, the state Senate is led by Tom Bakk, who represents the Arrowhead region, and he was a key player in the fight for medical cannabis. The compromise that was finally enacted in 2014 was the most restrictive in the nation, but was a foot in the door for the eventual decriminalization of marijuana.

15

LEGAL MEDICAL CANNABIS – THE FIRST STEP

"I support the bill." That's what our state senator for Lake County, Tom Bakk, wrote to me when I urged him to legalize medical marijuana in Minnesota. Senate File 1641 would have done just that, in exempting patients with AIDS, cancer, nausea, and many other conditions from criminal penalties for using cannabis prescribed by a doctor. Sen. Bakk, who is majority leader, pushed the bill through the Senate with a bipartisan vote of 48 to 18.

Our state representative, David Dill, was less enthusiastic. "I really don't think the bill is going anywhere," he told me, though "I could be wrong." As it turned out, he was partly right. The Senate bill didn't go anywhere, but the House of Representatives did pass (89 to 40) a much more limited compromise bill, S.F. 2470. The Senate agreed to the compromise, and Governor Mark Dayton signed it into law. Sen. Scott Dibble of Minneapolis and Rep. Carly Melin of Hibbing were instrumental in getting it passed. David Dill voted for the bill, but our other representative, Mary Murphy, voted against it.

What is the difference between what the Senate wanted and what eventually became law? Here are a few highlights:

1. The Senate bill would have made about 35,000 Minnesotans eligible to use medical cannabis. The House bill (the one signed into law) will only help about 5,000 patients.
2. The Senate bill would have made the drug available at up to 55 dispensaries statewide. The House bill permits only two

      manufacturers with 4 distribution points each, 8 for the entire state.

3. The House bill requires patients and their doctors to participate in an onerous and costly study.
4. The House bill leaves out patients with intractable pain, but does include cancer, glaucoma, AIDS, Tourette syndrome, Crohn's disease, ALS, and seizures. It also includes "chronic pain," wasting, and nausea if they are connected to cancer or terminal illness.
5. Under the House bill, patients will have to pay an annual fee of $200 to the state.

Law enforcement groups lobbied against the Senate bill. They apparently were afraid that the longer list of medical conditions might result in some people using the drug for enjoyment instead of for treatment. Actually, the law as passed does not permit smoking the weed; people can only use extracts of the plant in the form of pills or liquid. Of all the 21 states that have legalized medical marijuana so far, Minnesota is the only state with this restriction against natural herbal cannabis.

Nonetheless, supporters of the bill rejoiced after even the limited bill got through the legislature. They cited many cases of terrible suffering that standard medicines have not been able to help, but that can be successfully treated with marijuana. Some legislators who had opposed the bill changed their minds after hearing testimony from people with terrible pain or vomiting who have had to buy the drug illegally.

According to a new survey from Pew Research Center, a majority of Americans (54%) now support ending marijuana prohibition altogether. And 75% of those polled think that the sale and use of marijuana will eventually be legal nationwide. Further, 69% of Americans agree that alcohol is more harmful than marijuana. No one, in fact, has ever died from a marijuana overdose.

Here in Minnesota, the legislature decriminalized possession of a small amount of marijuana many years ago. The law here (and in 17 other states) treats it like a parking ticket – a small fine, no jail, and not classified as a "crime." Now it's time for us to consider following the lead of Washington and Colorado and take this victimless crime off the books entirely.

Like every other city in America, the city councils in Lake County's two cities (Two Harbors and Silver Bay) were forced to think about prayer after the U.S. Supreme Court decided <u>Town of Greece v. Gallaway</u>. There were sharp differences of opinion here, some saying that the First Amendment should prohibit government sponsored prayer at city council meetings, and others saying "we need more prayer in this country." As a former President of the American Civil Liberties Union of Minnesota, you know where I stand.

16

GOVERNMENT SPONSORED PRAYER IS NOW LEGAL

The United States Supreme Court, by a 5 to 4 vote, has now ruled that a city council may open its meetings with a prayer. A Christian prayer. Does that mean that we'll soon be hearing prayers at local council meetings?

There are different opinions in Silver Bay. City Administrator Lana Fralich says that council meetings are opened with the Pledge of Allegiance, not with prayer. "We keep people's individual religion to themselves, and we deal with <u>government</u>," she said. On the other hand, Mayor Joanne Johnson told me "I think this Supreme Court decision is a positive step forward. We need more prayer in this country."

As for Two Harbors, City Administrator Lee Klein says that "personally, I believe in separation of church and state." Mayor Randy Bolen could not be reached for comment.

The Supreme Court previously ruled (in 1987) that the Nebraska legislature could open each session with a prayer. However, Chief Justice Warren Burger noted that the prayers in that case were "non-sectarian" and that all references to Christ had been removed from the prayers.

In the 2014 case, however, almost all the prayers at the town council meetings in Greece, N.Y., were specifically Christian. Some elaborated on Christian theology, discussing "the saving sacrifice of Jesus Christ on the cross" and "the plan of redemption that is fulfilled in Jesus Christ." The audience was often asked to join in saying the "Our Father" prayer and bowing their heads.

For four months in 2007, after complaints by some residents, the town of Greece, N.Y., invited clergy from other religions to give the prayer. A Jewish man, a Baha'i leader, and a Wiccan priestess who invoked Apollo and Athena were among those who said the prayers. But then for the next 18 months the board reverted to inviting only Christian clergy.

Justice Anthony Kennedy, writing for the majority of the Supreme Court last month, came up with a new test for what violates the constitution's establishment clause – whether the prayers are "coercive." He said there was no evidence that "town board members directed the public to participate in the prayers, singled out dissidents for opprobrium, or indicated that their decisions might be influenced by a person's acquiescence in the prayer opportunity. No such thing occurred in the town of Greece."

Joining Kennedy in the outcome were Chief Justice John Roberts and Justices Antonin Scalia, Clarence Thomas, and Samuel Alito. It is interesting to note that all five were appointed by Republican presidents; and that all five are Roman Catholics.

The four dissenters were Justices Elena Kagan, Ruth Bader Ginsburg, Stephen Breyer, and Sonia Sotomayor, all appointed by Democratic presidents, and all Jewish (except Sotomayor, who is Catholic). Justice Kagan said that "When the citizens of this country approach their government, they do so only as Americans, not as members of one faith or another. And that means that even in a partly legislative body, they should not confront government-sponsored worship that divides them along religious lines … The Town of Greece betrayed that promise."

After the decision was announced, the American Civil Liberties Union (ACLU) commented that "Official religious favoritism should be off-limits under the Constitution. Town-sponsored sectarian prayer violates the basic rule requiring the government to stay neutral on matters of faith." On the other hand, the Alliance Defending Freedom praised the ruling, saying that "Speech censors should have no power to silence volunteers who pray for their communities just as the Founders did."

According to Erwin Chemerinsky, Professor of First Amendment Law at the University of California, this new "coercion" test seems to mean that a town could declare itself to be Christian (or any religion) because that would not coerce religious participation. And certainly if the majority of City Council members were Muslim, they can now open every meeting with Muslim prayers.

President James Madison, who helped write the Bill of Rights, made the following comment in 1822: "Religion Flourishes in greater purity, without than with the aid of Government." He even objected to appointment of a chaplain in the First Congress, for fear that they might one day appoint a Catholic chaplain: "To say that his principles are obnoxious or that his sect is small, is to lift the veil at once and exhibit in its native deformity the doctrine that religious truth is to be tested by numbers, or that the major sects have a right to govern the minor."

The Supreme Court has now taken a big step toward tearing down Jefferson's wall of separation between church and state.

Same-sex marriage has been debated in Minnesota for years. The first case in America to consider the issue was decided in Minnesota in 1971 (<u>Baker v. Nelson</u>), ruling that "marriage" is limited to persons of the opposite sex. But in 2014 that changed when the legislature adopted and Gov. Dayton signed a law permitting same sex couples to marry in Minnesota. It's a big step forward.

SAME-SEX MARRIAGE COMES TO MINNESOTA

On August 1, 2014, it became legal in Lake County for same-sex couples to marry. In fact, if you go to the Court House in Two Harbors to apply for a marriage license, the form now asks for the names of "First Applicant" and "Second Applicant" instead of "Bride" and "Groom."

Minnesota has now joined California, Connecticut, Delaware, Iowa, Maine, Maryland, Massachusetts, New Hampshire, New York, Rhode Island, Vermont, Washington, and Washington D.C. in permitting same-sex marriage. The total population now living in states with marriage equality is 95 million – almost one-third of the total U.S. population.

And we forget that this sudden change is not just a U.S. phenomenon. Queen Elizabeth – hardly a social radical – signed into law a bill legalizing same-sex marriages in England and Wales. The bill was backed by all three major political parties. In fact, it was Prime Minister David Cameron, leader of the tradition-minded Conservatives, who proposed the legislation in the first place.

Thus England and Wales join the fifteen countries (Argentina, Belgium, Brazil, Canada, Denmark, France, Iceland, Netherlands, New Zealand, Norway, Portugal, Spain, South Africa, Sweden, and Uruguay) that have passed legislation allowing same-sex couples to marry. The total population now living in countries with marriage-for-all is 641 million (9% of the world's people). A year ago, it was 289 million.

Polls show that about fifty-five per cent of the American people now support same-sex marriage. It seems certain that this percentage will increase every day until the entire United States joins the list of countries that grant marriage equality. Indeed, in his dissent to the Supreme Court decision invalidating the Defense of Marriage Act, Justice Scalia wrote that "the real rationale of today's opinion is that DOMA is motivated by a bare ... desire to harm couples in same-sex marriages ... How easy it is, indeed how inevitable, to reach the same conclusion with regard to state laws denying same-sex couples marital status."

Besides bringing about greater social acceptance of same-sex couples, these changes in the law also carry financial benefits under the Social Security and Medicare laws. As Jennifer Waters pointed out in the Wall Street Journal (July 14), "Gay and lesbian couples will be eligible for valuable spousal and survivor benefits that could be worth tens, maybe hundreds, of thousands of dollars to each household." President Barack Obama has promised that all relevant federal benefits and obligations will be implemented "swiftly and smoothly," including retirement and health benefits.

Thus we will continue moving forward into a better future.

Kathy Ogle (L) and Val Ulstad (R)
Protho Credit: Nathanael Kuenzli/Micaella Penning

One of the first same sex marriages in Minnesota was celebrated on the North Shore. Grand Marais, the county seat of Cook County, is a favorite spot for weddings because of its beautiful lake side location and vibrant touristy downtown. Now the local merchants, photographers, and restaurants are preparing to become a mecca for same sex couples who want to wed in one of the world's most beautiful places.

18

KATHY AND VAL: HAPPILY MARRIED AT LAST

It has now been over a year since same-sex marriage became legal in Minnesota (August 1, 2013). So far at least 2,934 same-sex couples have wed in cities and towns across Minnesota, according to statistics compiled by the Minneapolis Star Tribune. In Hennepin County about 25% of marriage licenses have been issued to same-sex couples since August 1.

In Lake County the numbers are much smaller, of course. Only four same-sex couples have received marriage licenses here, 11% of the 35 licenses issued since the law changed. However, in Cook County 14 of the 39 licenses issued have been to same-sex couples (36%).

I spoke with two women who got married in Cook County last fall. Val Ulstad and Kathy Ogle have been together for 31 years and say it was "a joy to finally be able to do what everybody else does when they're in love." Both of them are medical doctors, a cardiologist and an oncologist, who met at the University of Minnesota Medical School and worked at Hennepin County Medical Center and other clinics. Now they have left clinical practice and are running a consulting business that teaches leadership development (www.cascadebluff.net). For years they have spent part of each year at their cabin on the North Shore of Lake Superior.

Being married, they say, allows them "to participate in the path people choose," just as heterosexual couples do. But they point out that it also gives them many legal rights and responsibilities they were previously denied. They mention inheriting social security benefits, filing joint income tax returns, and visiting each other in the hospital.

A study conducted by Professor Anthony Winer and others at William Mitchell College of Law found 515 Minnesota statutes that provide rights and assign responsibilities to couples based on the legal definition of marriage. For example, an individual cannot be compelled to testify against their spouse in court (Minn. St. 595.02). A surviving spouse is entitled to sue for wrongful death (Minn. St. 466.05). A married person has responsibility for financial support for a spouse; responsibility for decisions relating to medical care and treatment; priority to be conservator, guardian, or personal representative for a spouse; the ability to inherit property from a spouse without a written will; the ability to insure a spouse; survivor benefits under workers' compensation laws and government pensions; and presumptions of parentage for children born during the marriage. Marriage also provides for an orderly process for divorce, parenting time, and property division if the couple splits up. See http://project515.org

The U.S. Supreme Court case that struck down the federal Defense of Marriage Act (U.S. v. Windsor) involved a same-sex couple (Edith Windsor and Thea Spyer) who married one another in Canada in 2007. Spyer died in 2009 and left her estate to Windsor. The IRS hit Windsor with an estate tax of $363,000, refusing to recognize their marriage. The Supreme Court ruled that the DOMA definition of marriage as solely between opposite-sex couples was a denial of equal protection and unconstitutional under the Due Process Clause of the 5th Amendment. The IRS therefore had to treat Windsor like any other surviving spouse, and could not levy an estate tax against her.

I asked Kathy and Val if people on the North Shore treat them as they would any other married couple, and they say people here have been very accepting. In fact, they like the North Shore so much they plan to make it their permanent home.

Last fall the Highway 61 magazine published an article about Val and Kathy, pointing out that "now that more Minnesotans are able to get married, businesses providing services for weddings – lodging establishments, restaurants, caterers, photographers, florists and more – may be busier than ever." "People love to get married on the North Shore," said photographer Jess Oullis. And if Val and Kathy are any indication, people also love to live on the North Shore.

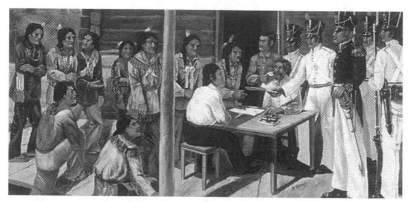

Caddo Indian Treaty of Cession, July 1, 1835. Mural in Louisiana
State Exhibit Museum, Shreveport, courtesy of Louisiana
Department of Culture, Recreation, and Tourism.

We all know about the United States government's shameful treatment of Native Americans. Treaties were made, Indians left their land in exchange for solemn promises, and then the "great white father" in Washington broke the promises. The Treaty of 1854 with the Chippewa Nation was an example of that. Now Congressman Rick Nolan, who represents the Arrowhead region in Washington, has pushed through a bill that will rectify a 160 year old injustice.

19

FOND DU LAC BAND TO SWAP LAND

We all know that the United States Congress passed very little legislation in 2013 and 2014. The Republican controlled House of Representatives voted nearly 50 times to repeal the Affordable Care Act (Obamacare), but didn't get around to doing much else. Only 65 laws were enacted by this "do-nothing Congress," the least productive ever.

One exception was a bill oddly named the "Fond du Lac Band of Lake Superior Chippewa Non-Intercourse Act of 2013." The Republicans and Democrats in the House and Senate got together and unanimously approved the bill – by voice vote. Here's the story:

One Hundred Sixty years ago (1854), two years after the big Sioux Uprising in southern Minnesota, the United States government entered into a treaty with the Chippewa Nation in our part of Minnesota. The treaty set aside 101,000 acres of land in Carlton County exclusively for the Fond du Lac Band Reservation. However, as happened so often with such treaties, the United States did not keep its end of the bargain. Homesteaders and others were wrongly allowed to settle on this land, taking ownership away from the Chippewa Band. Many of these settlers later failed to pay their real estate taxes, and eventually much of this land was forfeited to Carlton County.

An agreement has now been reached between Carlton County and the Chippewa Band to trade some 3,200 acres the County owns (tax-forfeited land) for 1,451 acres the Band owns outside its Reservation. The land exchange is of equal value on both sides. However, the deal requires the approval of Congress.

That's where our newly-elected Congressman, Rick Nolan, comes in. He introduced the bill to authorize the Band to make the land exchange. His bill was referred to the Committee on Natural Resources, a hearing was held, and the bill was unanimously approved by the Committee. The bill went to the floor of the House of Representatives and was unanimously approved. The bill then went to the Senate, where a companion bill was sponsored by Sen. Al Franken, and was passed unanimously. President Obama signed the bill into law on March 21, 2014.

According to Rep. Nolan, this bill will allow the Chippewa Band space to construct much-needed housing for its 6,700 members, as well as expand land for traditional hunting and gathering. And Carlton County will have valuable new timber and forestry resources. The present checkerboard of ownership on the Reservation will be corrected, allowing both the Band and the County to effectively manage the lands they control. Nolan's speech on the floor of the House can be watched at http://www.youtube.com/watch?v=DJskK8-jPbQ&feature=c4-overview&list=UUmGkPQXVR8GzVAPXN54AoXg

Passage of this bill will, at least in part, help to rectify the broken treaty of 1854. It's about time!

Green funerals are new here in Lake County. In fact, no cemetery here is yet willing to participate. All of them require a concrete vault and an embalmed body. But the Minnesota legislature has made other options available. Personally, I want to take advantage of them.

20

Green Funerals are now an Option

Last week a friend told me his father died, and he had to be embalmed before the public viewing and cremation. It didn't make sense to him to fill the body with embalming fluid and then burn it a couple of days later. He asked me if this was required by Minnesota law.

The answer, thanks to a recent change in the law, is NO. A group of citizens got behind the "Home Care of Our Deceased – Family Rights Legislation," helped move it through the legislature, and it was signed into law by Gov. Pawlenty in 2010.

The Minnesota Threshold Network was started by four home funeral educators in the fall of 2008. Soon others interested in conscious dying, after-death care, home funerals, home vigils, and green burials were meeting regularly. They thought the Minnesota law that required embalming for a public viewing of a body, prohibited minors from being in the presence of an unembalmed body, and restricted a family's transportation options was unreasonable.

They asked Representative Carolyn Laine and Senator Sandy Pappas to sponsor a bill. Knowing that funeral directors would raise objections based on the belief that unembalmed bodies pose a public health threat, Rep. Laine asked Dr. Michael Osterholm, Director of the Center for Infectious Disease Research at the University of Minnesota, for his support. He testified at the legislative hearings that unembalmed bodies do NOT normally pose a public health threat.

Another witness at the hearings was Minneapolis psychotherapist Heather Halen, who described how she had washed and dressed her deceased husband's body at home, and, using dry ice, kept him on the cool front porch for two days in a coffin friends had made. She told how comforting it was to have her husband's body close at hand, and to sit and talk to him during the awful, lonely first two nights after his death, something that could not have occurred had he been in a funeral parlor. Heather's testimony was so compelling that KSTP-TV ran a feature news story on it, highlighting the psychological, environmental, and economic advantages of caring for one's own at death.

Thanks to the change in the law, Minnesotans can now have public visitations of their unembalmed loved ones, minors may view the body, and families have more options regarding the transportation of a body. Green funerals, in which no embalming takes place and a body is buried without any toxic material being introduced to the earth, are legal. Natural burials also avoid metal and hardwood coffins, concrete burial vaults, and marble headstones.

Minnesota is also leading the way in "green cremation," a flameless process of reducing a body to its basic elements using alkaline hydrolysis. The Mayo Clinic Medical School has been using hydrolysis in its body donor program for several years, and now the first commercial unit in the U.S. has opened in Stillwater, MN.

Rep. Carolyn Laine, along with my sister Nancy Manahan, both members of the Minnesota Threshold Network, have spoken on these developments to large audiences at the Two Harbors Library and the Silver Bay Library. Nancy wrote the award-winning memoir *Living Consciously, Dying Gracefully: A Journey with Cancer and Beyond*. Her wife and co-author, Becky Bohan, contributed information for this article.

Lake County deals with social ills

Family violence occurs in Lake County, of course, and in every county in the world. But Lake County is doing something about it by coordinating the response among all the agencies involved – law enforcement, County Attorney, Victim Witness Coordinator, judge, and probation.

21

VIOLENCE AGAINST WOMEN (AND MEN) IN LAKE COUNTY

Most people haven't heard of the Coordinated Community Response Team (CCRT) here in Lake County – it's only two years old. Every month representatives of numerous agencies in the county get together to coordinate their response to sexual assault and domestic violence.

When a rape or sexual assault occurs, the hospital Emergency Department is often the first place where the victim seeks help. So Lake View Hospital has developed a Sexual Assault Nurse Examiner (SANE) program. This is coordinated with law enforcement officers – the Sheriff, Two Harbors police, and Silver Bay Police – on the CCRT.

Then the victim may seek help from the Lake County Health and Human Services office. The County Attorney will be involved if criminal charges are filed against the perpetrator, as will the Victim Witness Coordinator, the judge, and the probation officer (if the perpetrator is convicted). All of these people are also members of the Coordinated Community Response Team.

Rachel Johnson, a sexual assault advocate at North Shore Horizons in Two Harbors, facilitates the meetings of the CCRT. Two years ago North Shore Horizons got a grant from the Woman's Foundation of Minnesota, which helped get CCRT up and running. Laura Comrie from Lake View Hospital has worked on the idea from the nurse's standpoint for some time, and has received specialized training. Now the group is developing a "protocol" that spells out exactly what should be done (best practices) when a sexual assault occurs.

According to the protocol, "sexual assault victims have the right to immediate, compassionate and comprehensive medical-legal evaluation and treatment by a specially trained professional." The goals of SANE are to protect the victim from further harm, to provide forensic evidence collection (when the victim chooses to pursue a medical exam), to evaluate and treat any sexually transmitted infections, to evaluate pregnancy risk and offer prevention, to refer victims for medical care and counseling, and to enhance the ability of law enforcement agencies to successfully prosecute sexual assault cases.

A similar but unrelated effort called "The Duluth Model" has been operating in Duluth since 1980. They coordinate all types of services when violence occurs against women, including Orders for Protection and batterer intervention programs. The Duluth Model has been copied all over the world and has won many awards for coordinated community response to domestic assault. In fact, in 2014 the Duluth Model was named the best domestic abuse intervention program **in the world** by the World Future Council, the Inter-Parliamentary Union (IPU), and U.N. Women.

Last year in Minnesota 37 people died in domestic violence homicides – 24 women and 7 men were murdered by a current or former intimate partner. Also, 6 friends and family members were murdered, and 12 minor children were left without parents. A wonderful book called *Half the Sky* by Nicholas Kristof and his wife Sheryl WuDunn describes the abuse of women all over the world in moving terms and offers solutions that make me hopeful that the terrible crimes against women can be reduced.

Four years ago Kay Marie Sisto was murdered by her husband in Duluth. In order to remember her and all the others who die each year from domestic violence, there is an annual 5K walk/run/roll on the Western Waterfront Trail and the Willard Munger Trail. The registration fee is used to support Domestic Abuse Intervention Programs.

And here in Lake County there is an annual fund raiser for North Shore Horizons, whose goal is to help survivors of violence (domestic and sexual abuse). It is held at Superior Shores and features gourmet food donated by many North Shore restaurants.

Do victims of crimes have rights too? In Minnesota they do, with a whole chapter in the statute book (Minn. St. 611A) listing the rights. In Lake County I am the Victim Witness Coordinator and it is my job to see that victims' rights are respected.

22

THE VICTIM/WITNESS COORDINATOR IS HERE TO HELP YOU

It used to be that when a crime was committed, the victim had no rights. The law was focused on protecting the rights of the alleged criminal – the right to remain silent, the right to a lawyer, the presumption of innocence, the right to a speedy trial. The victim was just another witness to the alleged crime.

For the past 30 years that has no longer been true in Minnesota. Every county in the state now has a Victim/Witness Coordinator.

Here are some of the rights that crime victims have in Minnesota:

- The right to a copy of the police report (at no cost) in domestic abuse cases
- The right not to be required to take a polygraph exam (lie detector)
- The right to be notified if the prosecutor decides not to file charges
- The right to attend all court hearings in the case
- The right to receive notice of all court hearings, including sentencing
- The right to request a speedy trial
- The right not to disclose their address in open court
- The right to a secure waiting area during court
- The right to bring a supportive person to court

- The right not to be disciplined or fired by their employer if called to testify in court, or if attending any hearing in the case of a violent crime
- The right to receive a witness fee and be reimbursed for lost wages, childcare, meals, and accommodations
- The right to object to a proposed disposition or sentence
- The right to know about any plea bargain agreements
- The right to have input in a pretrial diversion program decision
- The right to inform the judge at the sentencing of the impact the crime has had on them
- The right to know what was the final disposition of the case
- The right to be told about any transfer of the offender from prison or jail, as well as any escape and apprehension
- The right to apply for financial assistance from the Crime Victims Reparations Board for payment of expenses related to physical or psychological injury from a violent crime
- The right to receive restitution as a part of the sentence, to have a civil judgment entered against the defendant (at no cost), and to request a probation review hearing if the restitution has not been paid
- The right to enroll in the Safe at Home program and have a secret address

And finally, the right to be notified about all of these rights! It has been a huge improvement in the way our court system treats victims, and Minnesota has been a national leader. It was just 10 years ago that Congress passed the landmark Crimes Victims' Rights Act of 2004 (18 U.S.C. §3771), extending many of these rights to victims in federal criminal cases.

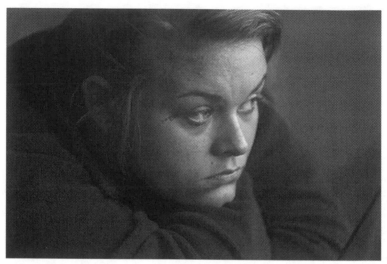

Bobbi Larson

STAR TRIBUNE MINNEAPOLIS – ST. PAUL 2014

Prostitution has long been recognized as a victimless crime, but it is nonetheless a crime. So women and girls who engage in prostitution are arrested and prosecuted just as any criminal would be. But isn't a juvenile in "the life" more of a victim than a criminal? The john who pays her for sex is preying on a minor, someone who needs social services, schooling, and a home, rather than jail. A young woman from Two Harbors has focused national attention on this truth.

23

Bobbi and the Safe Harbor Law

Bobbi Larson of Two Harbors recently allowed the Minneapolis Star Tribune to report her history of being a victim of child sex trafficking. Local people, she says, are calling her now to tell her "I'm proud of you."

Many adolescent girls in Minnesota and throughout the country are lured into prostitution by pimps who take advantage of their emotional vulnerability. Until now these girls have been subject to arrest and prosecution as juvenile delinquents. However, Minnesota's new "Safe Harbor" law recognizes that these children are victims, not criminals.

Bobbi was lucky, since she has a loving family in Two Harbors who welcomed her home after she was victimized. Many girls, however, come from broken or hostile homes and police have no place to send them after rescuing them from the sex trade.

The Minnesota legislature in 2014 appropriated $2.8 million to fund the Safe Harbor law, $1 million of which went to create shelters for sex trafficking victims. Construction soon began on a new shelter in St. Paul that will be able to house 12 victims, and four other organizations have been awarded grants across the state. At the groundbreaking in St. Paul, Mayor Chris Coleman said "Today is a gigantic leap forward. We're not going to allow our children to be exploited." Girls ages 10 to 17 will be able to stay at the shelter up to three months and can receive chemical dependency treatment, mental health help, and vocational training.

Also included in the funding is money for training law enforcement officers across the state to more effectively understand and work with victims.

U.S. Senator Amy Klobuchar has introduced a bill called the Stop Exploitation Through Trafficking Act (SETT), aimed at getting all states to enact Safe Harbor laws like Minnesota's, ensuring that minors who are trafficked are treated as victims.

According to the Women's Foundation of Minnesota, criminalizing the victim not only causes them further harm; it offers a weak and ineffective response to traffickers' manipulative and sophisticated grooming and control. The average age a child enters prostitution, they say, is about 12 to 13 years of age – that's 6th and 7th graders. Furthermore, a victim-centered response saves taxpayer money; one study shows a savings of $34 tax dollars for every $1 invested in victim-centered models.

Here's what the new Minnesota law (effective August 1, 2014) says: "The term delinquent child does not include a child alleged to have engaged in conduct which would, if committed by an adult, violate any federal, state, or local law relating to being hired, offering to be hired, or agreeing to be hired by another individual to engage in sexual penetration or sexual conduct."

Last year President Obama declared January as National Slavery and Human Trafficking Prevention Month. As he put it, human trafficking is "one of the greatest human rights abuses of our time." It's a crime, he said, that "amounts to modern-day slavery."

Surely there are no people in Lake County who live on the street, in sheds, or in their car – it's too cold here! But this assumption is wrong. I was shocked to discover the truth.

24

ARE THERE HOMELESS PEOPLE HERE?

Are there homeless people in Lake County, Minnesota? I haven't seen anyone sleeping under bridges, living in cardboard boxes, or lying on the sidewalk in sleeping bags (as can be seen in big cities).

However, the answer to the question is YES, according to Tara Golden, director of North Shore Horizons in Two Harbors. She says there are two types of homelessness here.

Some of the homeless people in Lake County are not very visible. Their home has been foreclosed, or they've lost their job and can't pay the rent, or their wage earning spouse has left them. They are living now (at least temporarily) in a hunting shack, a tent, an ice house, a car, or on a couch in a friend's or relative's home. We don't notice them.

But another type of homeless person has left their home because it is not safe to remain. These people, who are victims of domestic violence or sexual assault, are also homeless according to Golden, and need to find safe housing.

Some of these are fleeing their abuser and need crisis housing. Last year there were such victims from ten households in Lake County (13 adults and 3 children) whom North Shore Horizons placed in crisis safe housing, usually for two or three days. This gave the victims time to report crimes to the police (if they wished), get an Order for Protection (if they wished), and make more permanent living arrangements. But Golden says that another 177 adults and 116 children, victims of domestic or sexual violence, sought services last year but did not ask for emergency housing.

North Shore Horizons has room for some of these homeless people on a longer term basis, including six apartments next to their office in Two Harbors and three offsite units. These range from two bedroom units that are transitional (up to 2 years), two or three bedroom units that are available for up to 5 years, and smaller apartments that can be permanent housing for people with a disabling condition. All those who are helped are victims of domestic violence or sexual assault in Lake County, and must meet low income guidelines. The rent is subsidized – tenants pay 30% of their adjusted gross income as rent, and the balance is paid by grants from the federal government (HUD), the Housing and Redevelopment Authority of Two Harbors (HRA), the Hearth Connection, and the Arrowhead Economic Opportunity Agency (AEOA)(which gets a grant from HUD).

Last year North Shore Horizons placed people from 14 households (18 adults and 16 children) in transitional or permanent housing. However, they had to turn away 62 homeless adults and 62 children for lack of space.

According to the Minnesota Housing Partnership, a family in Lake County must earn at least $12.42 an hour to afford a modest two bedroom apartment and not pay over 30% of their income for rent and utilities. See http://mhponline.org/images/stories/docs/research/reports/out_of_reach_minnesota_2014.pdf

That's more than the $9.50 minimum wage that the Legislature just approved, and leaves a lot of people out – 52% of renters in Lake County can't afford to rent a two bedroom apartment unless they work on average 69 hours a week.

Recently the Duluth City Council unanimously passed a "Homeless Bill of Rights." It states that all people, including the homeless, are guaranteed "freedom from discrimination in education, employment, public services, public accommodations, movement, worship, speech and participation in the democratic process regardless of housing status." Further, "everyone has the right to a standard of living adequate for … health and well-being … including food, clothing and housing."

The Minnesota Legislature is working on a bill that would grant $100,000,000 for affordable housing in the state. "It's a cost to society to have 14,000 homeless Minnesotans on any given night," Rep. Alice Hausman, DFL-St. Paul, the bill's author, said. "There are moral and compassionate issues to fighting homelessness. But it's also a dollars-and-cents issue." "The bonding bill has to gain the approval of a supermajority — 60 percent in the House — to pass, and that isn't going to be easy," Hausman said. If passed, funding would be awarded by the Minnesota Housing Finance Agency through a competitive grant process.

Nearly half of Minnesota's homeless population — people who do not have permanent places to stay — are people under 21, according to a Wilder Foundation study. It's time for Minnesota to extend a helping hand to them. After all, it's not a crime to be homeless.

COURT PROCEDURES
IN LAKE COUNTY

eFiling may not seem like an important topic, but Lake County is one of the pioneers in Minnesota that will soon make paper obsolete in the court system.

LAKE COUNTY COURT IS eFILING PIONEER

Out of 87 counties in Minnesota, eleven have started a 21st century experiment. Two of these eleven are Lake and Cook Counties (known as "The Shore"). Our court is a pioneer in the use of eFiling.

In civil and family cases, no longer can attorneys simply mail their lawsuits, affidavits, and briefs to the judge or the court administrator. Those papers must be put into PDF format, served by computer on the other parties' attorneys, and then filed by computer with the court. Paper no longer exists in Lake and Cook Counties for these cases.

In addition to mandatory eFiling in civil and family cases, attorneys can voluntarily eFile in adoption, criminal, probate, and juvenile cases in Lake and Cook Counties.

And after all the bugs have been worked out, electronic filing will be mandatory in all 87 counties. The vision announced by the Supreme Court is that "Minnesota courts will operate in an electronic information environment … All cases will be eFiled or submitted on paper and converted to electronic images." The goals are to "increase productivity and reduce operational costs," "build a sound and secure technical infrastructure," and "facilitate culture change from paper processes to electronic court processes." The benefits, according to the Supreme Court, are that litigants will be able to file case documents without going to the courthouse; judges and litigants "will be able to view and work with … documents even when someone else is viewing the case file"; and court records not considered confidential will be viewable anywhere in the state through the Judicial Branch Website.

At present, the mandatory eFiling requirements for "The Shore" courts do not apply to probate, mental health, adoption, child protection, conciliation court, juvenile, or criminal cases. Also, they don't apply to self-represented (pro se) litigants.

It should be noted that some documents can be filed as "confidential," such as medical records, social security numbers, and financial account numbers, so they will not be available for public inspection.

For more information, go to www.mncourts.gov/efile

Orders for Protection are an important tool when dealing with domestic violence. In Lake County, Judge Cuzzo has made some significant changes in the way they are handled. It will make the procedures easier and more fair for everyone, protecting the rights of both the Petitioner and the Respondent.

26

RULES FOR OFP HEARINGS ARE CHANGED

Minnesota has had a Domestic Abuse Act since 1979. This law authorizes judges to issue an Order for Protection (OFP) when there has been bodily harm, fear of bodily harm, terroristic threats, or criminal sexual conduct between family or household members. The law does not cover emotional or mental abuse. An OFP is a family court case, not a criminal case. The Minnesota Supreme Court has called it "a band-aid, designed to curtail the harm one household member may be doing to the other in the short term, until a more permanent dispute resolution can be put in place."

The procedure to get an OFP is as follows: The parties must be spouses or former spouses, parents and children, related by blood, have lived together, have a child together (born or unborn), or be involved in a romantic or sexual relationship. The abused person (the Petitioner) does not have to pay a filing fee to the court, nor sheriff fees to serve the papers on the abuser (the Respondent).

If immediate and present danger of further abuse is alleged, a temporary (ex parte) OFP is signed by the judge. Some years ago I asked the appellate courts to require notice to the Respondent before issuance of an OFP evicting him from his home. The Court of Appeals agreed, but the Minnesota Supreme Court disagreed, saying that "the risk of danger increases once the victim makes the choice or attempts to leave the abusive relationship." *Baker v. Baker*, 492 N.W.2d 282 (1992)

The ex parte order will forbid the Respondent from physically harming the Petitioner or any minor child(ren) in the home, and

Respondent may also be prohibited from entering the Petitioner's home or place of employment, having any contact, cancelling insurance coverage, or harming a pet. No court hearing is required unless one of the parties requests it, or if the Petitioner is asking for additional relief, such as temporary custody and visitation, temporary support, counseling, treatment, or possession of property.

If a hearing is held, it will typically be set within 7 days (if an ex parte order was given) or 14 days (if not). Here in Lake County, in the past that hearing was simply a chance to see if the parties agreed to the OFP, which can be for up to two years. If not, then another hearing was set a week or two later, at which both parties could present witnesses and evidence.

Judge Michael Cuzzo has now told me that he is changing that 2-step process in Lake and Cook Counties. Even though the scheduling will be more difficult, he will now try to hear the witnesses and make the decision at the first hearing, so there won't be any need for a second hearing. Several OFP cases are often set for hearing on the same day, but the judge says that normally only one or two are contested and require witnesses. Continuances will be granted, he said, "only under extreme circumstances."

Another local rule that Judge Cuzzo has put in place applies when the Petitioner has a change of heart and wants to dismiss the OFP. The judge says he will not consider such a request until five days have passed since the issuance of the OFP, and the Petitioner must submit a statement that he or she has met with Human Services, North Shore Horizons, the Victim/Witness Coordinator, or a mental health counselor, and has been apprised of available resources if he or she is subject to domestic violence in the future.

Recently I was involved in a case where the wife had gotten an OFP against the husband, and he was required to move out of the house. He asked for a hearing, and at the hearing the wife said she wanted the case dismissed and the OFP cancelled. However, Judge Cuzzo required her to meet first with Human Services, and after she did so she came back to court and said she had changed her mind. So the husband filed for divorce and in a short time he and she reached a permanent settlement. He got the house, she got the money, and she dismissed the OFP (after once again meeting with Human Services).

The Court Administrator has more information, available for free, about Orders for Protection.

Another tool in the arsenal for dealing with interpersonal violence and harassment is the HRO. Here I walk readers through what it is and how to obtain one in Lake County using online resources.

27

CAN I GET A HARASSMENT RESTRAINING ORDER?

You can learn a lot about legal matters, and get a lot of free forms, if you go to www.mncourts.gov.

First of all there's a box that says "Find Your Court," so click on "Lake County" and then on "GO." At the top in small print, click on "Court Forms." There are 34 categories of forms listed.

If you click on "Harassment" you will find a large number of forms. One of these is "Petitioner's Harassment Packet," which in turn contains four forms. The first one is an instruction sheet with a complete guide to getting a Harassment Restraining Order (HRO). In this guide we learn that a person who is a victim of harassment (Petitioner) may seek a restraining order from the Court. The parent or guardian of a minor who is the victim of harassment may seek a restraining order on behalf of the minor. The restraining order prohibits harassment and may be issued against an individual (Respondent) who has engaged in harassment, or against organizations that have sponsored or promoted harassment. A restraining order ends on the date specified in the order. This is usually two years from the date the order is signed.

Under Minnesota statutes, harassment is defined as follows:

1. A single incident of physical or sexual assault.
2. Repeated incidents of intrusive or unwanted acts, words or gestures that have a substantial adverse effect or are intended to have a substantial adverse effect on the safety, security or privacy

of another, regardless of the relationship between you and the alleged harasser.

3. Targeted residential picketing, which includes:
   a. marching, standing, or patrolling by one or more persons directed solely at a particular residential building in a manner that adversely affects the safety, security, or privacy of an occupant of the building, and
   b. marching, standing, or patrolling by one or more persons which prevents an occupant of a residential building from gaining access to or exiting from the property on which the residential building is located.

4. A pattern of attending public events after being notified that one's presence is harassing to another.

You just click on the form for "Petitioner's Affidavit and Petition," fill it out, and file it with the Court Administrator. You must pay a filing fee of $245.00 unless you meet low income guidelines, or the harassment falls under the Stalking statute for harassment. If you have alleged an immediate and present danger of harassment, the judge will issue an immediate temporary HRO. The Sheriff will serve the Petition and Order on the Respondent without charging you a fee.

The Respondent has a right to request a hearing to argue against the restraining order. Respondent must make this request within 20 days from service of the Petition, or within 45 days of the date of the Order if an immediate temporary HRO was issued (this inconsistency will no doubt be corrected by the Legislature next session). The hearing is normally held within 14 days.

If there is a hearing, both parties must testify, and if possible should bring witnesses and documents to support their case. If the judge rules in your favor and issues the HRO, it normally is valid for a period of two years.

You can get more information, specific to Lake County, at http://www.mncourts.gov/district/6/?page=1591. This page has some helpful suggestions that are not on the statewide page. For example, it says that in order to file you must have the full name and address of the person who is harassing you. You should bring a picture of the Respondent to the court when you file, if possible, as well as his/her work address (so he or she can be served with the Order). You should also bring written dates and notes concerning the harassment covering the last year (from the most recent incident going backwards). If the Respondent disobeys your HRO, you should call 911 immediately and make sure the police make a report – it is a crime to disobey an HRO.

The Court Administrator has more information, available for free, about Harassment Restraining Orders.

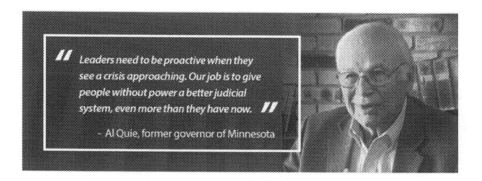

Leaders need to be proactive when they see a crisis approaching. Our job is to give people without power a better judicial system, even more than they have now.

- Al Quie, former governor of Minnesota

A bi-partisan task force, along with the Minnesota State Bar Association, has been trying to change the manner in which we select judges. So far their proposal hasn't gone anywhere, but it's a good idea to know what's being attempted. I'm hoping that the coalition will continue working on this in the next legislative session.

28

How Should We Choose Judges?

It was pretty amazing to see all the groups that got together recently to sponsor a meeting at the DECC in Duluth. The AFL-CIO and the Chamber of Commerce. The League of Women Voters, Common Cause, and the Bar Association. Former governors Al Quie (R), Wendell Anderson (D), and Arne Carlson (R). Former Chief Justices Kathleen Blatz, Sandy Keith, and Eric Magnuson, along with Justice Alan Page. All the big businesses in Minnesota (3M, Best Buy, BC/BS, Cargill, General Mills, Target, Medtronic, Microsoft, Xcel Energy). What issue could unite such a diverse group?

They call it the Coalition for Impartial Justice, and they want to change how we choose judges in Minnesota.

Judges have to run for election every six years, and right now any lawyer can run against a judge. In many states special interest groups have spent millions of dollars to get their own man elected. Just read John Grisham's novel _The Appeal_ for a scary scenario of what can (and did) happen. Look at recent million-dollar judicial elections in Wisconsin and Illinois.

Candidates for most elected offices run on platforms. They want better roads, more cops on the street, financial aid for farmers, and so on. But judge candidates have never had platforms – "I will give maximum sentences to all defendants" or "I will give custody of kids to fathers." We want judges who will be impartial and fair. Yet since the Supreme Court decided _Republican Party of Minnesota v. White_ (2002) and _Citizens United v. Federal Election Commission_ (2010), we now have the spectacle of unlimited money being spent on judicial candidates who have platforms.

The remedy? The coalition is proposing a constitutional amendment called the <u>Impartial Justice Act</u>. Instead of running against challengers, judges would run against their own record, and be voted up or down.

First, judges will be evaluated by a non-partisan commission appointed by all three branches of government, the majority of whom will be non-attorneys. Judges will be evaluated on standards including their integrity, impartiality, and knowledge of the law. Evaluations will be made available to the public, so voters know how their judges have performed.

Second, voters will decide whether to retain or replace a judge.

Third, if a judge is voted out, or a vacancy occurs, the governor will appoint the new judge. However, the appointment must be made from a list of three applicants chosen by the Judicial Selection Commission. We already use this Merit Selection system for district court judges, but the proposed law will include Court of Appeals and Supreme Court judges too.

I was a member of the Judicial Selection Commission for many years (appointed by the Minnesota Supreme Court), and I found the other members to be completely objective. I never even knew if they were Republican or Democrat – they just wanted to find and recommend to the Governor the three best persons available. If Minnesotans adopt this constitutional amendment, that is how all future judges will be chosen in Minnesota.

Photo Collection of the Supreme Court of the United States

Here's a bit of legal learning that doesn't have much to do with Lake County or the North Shore, other than the fact that the decisions of the conservative Roberts court have had a negative impact on every citizen in the United States.

29

U.S. SUPREME COURT AS LIBERAL AS PEOPLE THINK

The recent decision of the United States Supreme Court invalidating DOMA has led many to believe that the Court has become much more liberal, like a branch of the ACLU that now protects the rights of minorities. That case struck down the "Defense of Marriage Act," which limited federal marriage benefits to opposite sex couples, on the ground that the government cannot discriminate against same sex couples legally married in their state.

However, let's take a look at other recent decisions of the court. The majority of the nine justices are still eager to limit people's rights. Here are the 5 to 4 decisions:

In *Salinas v. Texas* the majority said that if you exercise your right to remain silent outside of an in-custody situation, your silence can be put into evidence at your trial and used against you.

In *Vance v. Ball State University,* the majority limited the right to sue for a supervisor's racial or sexual harassment, saying that a "supervisor" is not a boss who directs your work, but only a person who can hire or fire you.

In *University of Texas Southwestern Medical Center v. Nassar*, the majority imposed a more difficult standard for "retaliation" claims under the Civil Rights Act, rejecting long-standing interpretations by the EEOC.

In *Maryland v. King*, the majority ruled that the police can take DNA samples from you when you're arrested, even without a warrant or any basis for suspicion.

In *Shelby County v. Holder*, the majority invalidated part of the 1965 Voting Rights Act (which they had upheld four times previously) and said that preclearance of election changes in the Deep South are no longer necessary.

In *Clapper v. Amnesty International*, the majority threw out a lawsuit challenging the government's surveillance of citizens, saying that the plaintiffs could not show that <u>they</u> were spied on. Since the surveillance is secret, of course, that means that nobody can ever challenge it!

In *American Express Co. v. Italian Colors Restaurant*, the majority decided that American Express can prohibit class-action arbitration challenging its power to charge credit card fees 30 percent higher than anyone else, even though individual arbitrations would be way too expensive to be practical. Too bad for you, Mr. or Mrs. Consumer.

Who are the five men who made up this majority? In all but one case, they were Chief Justice John Roberts, Antonin Scalia, Anthony Kennedy, Clarence Thomas, and Samuel Alito. All 5 were appointed by Presidents Reagan, Bush I, or Bush II. The four dissenters were Ruth Bader Ginsburg, Stephen Breyer, Sonia Sotomayor, and Elena Kagan, appointed by Presidents Clinton or Obama. It is obvious that there is a huge and long-lasting difference in which President appoints Supreme Court Justices! The present conservative majority cannot be described as liberal, despite the DOMA decision.

Representative Rick Nolan

There is too much money in politics. Our elected representatives spend half their time raising money for the next election, instead of legislating. Well over half of the members of Congress are guaranteed reelection, because their gerrymandered districts are designed for one–party dominance. Voter ID laws and shortening times and places to vote make it harder for citizens to participate. Is there anything that can be done?

NOLAN WANTS TO "RESTORE DEMOCRACY"

Our Congressman, Rick Nolan, has introduced a Resolution in the Congress (Res. 695) to "Restore Democracy." That sounds pretty dramatic, and he means it to be. His idea is that our country has gone way off track and the government needs some fundamental restructuring.

Nolan wants to "change the way we do politics by ending the corrupt influence of big money in our elections, controlling the time we spend campaigning, making all 435 Congressional districts competitive, ending voter suppression, encouraging voter participation, and bringing democracy back to Congress itself." That's pretty ambitious.

His ideas have already gotten a lot of support. For example, Congressman John Conyers of Michigan, the Ranking Member and former Chairman of the House Judiciary Committee, is backing the bill, as is Congressman Alan Lowenthal of California. So are Public Citizen (Ralph Nader's group) and Common Cause (John Gardner's group), as well as a number of unions. For his news conference, go to http://nolan.house.gov/media-center/videos/ rep-nolan-holds-rally-to-restore-democracy

The **Restore Democracy Act** is a seven point blueprint, any piece of which would constitute major reform. Taken together, the plan would bring about a new golden age of bi-partisan democracy – a model for the world and a reaffirmation of our great American experience. In brief, the measure calls for the following:

1. **Overturning the U.S. Supreme Court's Citizens United decision**. Corporations are not 'people' and money is not 'free speech'.
2. **Establishing a public-private system of election financing** to empower small donors and make candidates answerable to the people rather than to wealthy special interests.
3. **Restricting spending on Congressional campaigns** to a period of 60 days before an election. Campaigning and raising money all year, every year is simply wrong.
4. **Prohibiting incumbents and challengers from raising money while Congress is in session.** (Minnesota and other states already apply this restriction to their legislatures.) Members of Congress need to go to Washington and govern – not raise money.
5. **Ending political gerrymandering of Congressional seats** to make all 435 competitive once again at election time. (Currently only about 35 districts fit that description.)
6. **Stopping voter suppression – and encouraging voter participation** with online voter registration in every state.
7. **Returning the U.S. House to a system of 'Regular Order.'** With the exception of national emergencies, that means no bill can be considered on the Floor of the House without having gone through the committee process under an 'open rule' – with amendments fully considered and given an up or down vote.

The bill has been referred to the House Subcommittee on the Constitution and Civil Justice, and also to the House Administration and House Rules Committees. They will study it to death. In the opinion of www.govtrack.us, it has a 0% chance of getting past committee and a 0% chance of passing. Why should this be? Are our elected representatives so vested in continuing the current dysfunctional system that they won't even allow Nolan's ideas to come to a vote on the floor?

The current Congress is the most unaccomplished in history, with fewer bills passed and less ability to function that ever before. Unless citizens make their voices heard loudly on Capitol Hill, and unless Nolan's bill becomes something we all talk about, things will continue as they have in recent times.